Contents

Plus...

The poster shows you what safari animals look like in real life.

Add the colourful eye stickers to your crafts.

The templates will help you draw the shapes needed for some of the projects.

HOW to use this book

Do you like making things? Are you an animal lover?

Then you'll love the 15 fun projects in this book. Read the instructions carefully and ask an adult if you need help.

Symbols

✋ This tells you if you need to ask an adult for help.

⏱ This tells you how long the project will take, once you have collected the equipment.

✂ This tells you how difficult the project is. ★ is the easiest and ★★★ is the most difficult.

Before you start!

- Clear a surface to work on and cover it with newspaper.
- Wear an apron or old t-shirt to protect your clothing.
- Gather all the equipment you need.

You will need

The equipment should be easy to find, around the house or from a craft store. Always ask before using materials from home.

cheetah

Give a friend a fright with this bright pop-out card!

✋ Some help needed

⏱ 30 minutes

✂ ★★

YOU WILL NEED

- 🐾 Card – thin green (A4), thin yellow, yellow strip (18 cm x 3 cm), scraps of assorted green
- 🐾 Coloured pencils
- 🐾 Eye stickers provided
- 🐾 Felt Pen – black
- 🐾 Glue stick
- 🐾 Pencil
- 🐾 Ruler
- 🐾 Scissors

1 Fold the green card in half. Cut out leaf shapes from scraps of green card and glue them onto the front and inside.

2 Make each tab 2 cm long

Fold the strip of yellow card in half, and fold tabs on each end. Stick the tabs inside the green card so the folds match up in the centre.

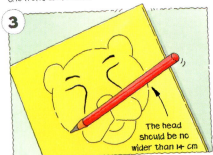

3 The head should be no wider than 14 cm

Use the template to draw the cheetah head and face outline on yellow card.

4 Draw the features with the black felt pen, then colour them in using coloured pencils. Add the eye stickers.

Numbered stages

Each stage of the project is numbered and illustrated. Follow the stages in the order shown to complete the project.

Safety!

If the symbols show 'Help needed', you must ask an adult for help before you begin. Be careful when using scissors, sharp pencils or glue.

5

Run a ruler along the fold to make it extra firm

Cut out the face. Fold it in half, making a firm crease down the centre.

6

Glue the head to the card strip, matching up all three folds in the centre. Leave to dry.

Finished project photo

At the end of each project, the photo shows what your craft should look like. Don't worry if it looks a bit different. Making things is about having fun!

Happy Birthday

write a special greeting on the front

SNARL!

Also make... a leopard

Follow the same steps, but give the big cat different features.

Also make...

With just a few simple changes, you can make fun variations of some crafts.

11

Elephant

Make a colourful gift tag to brighten up presents!

 Help not needed

 30 minutes

  ★

YOU WILL NEED

- Card – thick grey (A5), thick white
- Eye sticker provided
- Glue stick
- Hole punch
- Pencil
- Scissors
- Thread

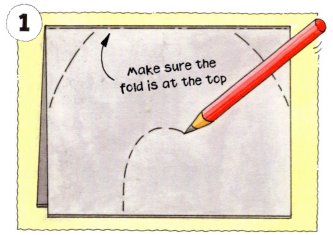

1 Make sure the fold is at the top

Fold a piece of grey card in half. Draw the outline of an elephant's body on it.

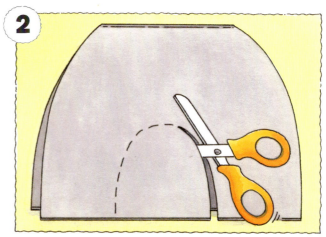

2

Cut out the shape. Do not cut along the folded edge.

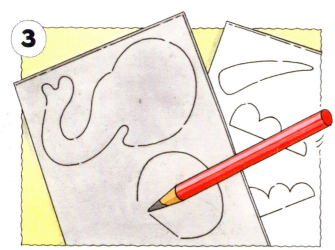

3

Using the templates, draw a head and ear on another piece of grey card. Draw a tusk and toes on the white card. Cut them out.

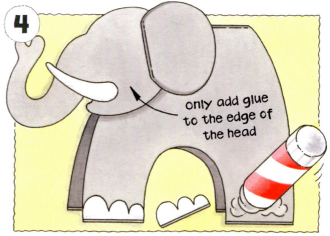

4 only add glue to the edge of the head

Add glue to the body parts and stick them on the elephant's body.

5

Add an eye sticker.

6

Use any colour for the thread

Punch a hole in the back of the body and attach the thread.

TRUMP! TRUMP! TRUMP!

Also make... different coloured gift tags, each with the trunk in a new position.

write your message inside

Flamingo

This birdy door sign will keep nosy beaks out of your room!

YOU WILL NEED

 Help not needed

 30 minutes, plus drying time

  ★★

- Acrylic paint – pink
- Bead – pink (2 cm in diameter)
- 2 buttons – large pink
- Eye stickers provided
- Felt pen – black
- Glue stick
- Paintbrush

- Paper – assorted pink
- Pencil (sharp)
- 4 pipe cleaners – thin pink
- Polystyrene craft ball (6 cm in diameter)
- Scissors

1 To make the body, paint the polystyrene craft ball with pink paint. Leave to dry.

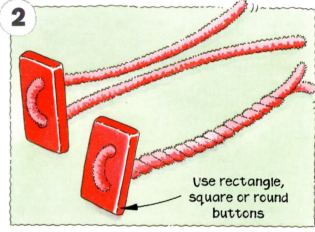

2 Use rectangle, square or round buttons

To make each leg, thread the end of a pipe cleaner through the button holes. Twist both halves of the pipe cleaner together.

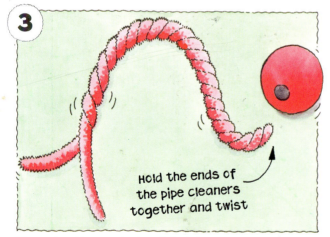

3 Hold the ends of the pipe cleaners together and twist

To make the neck, twist two pipe cleaners together. Push the bead onto one end.

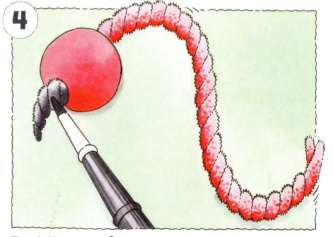

4 Twist the end of the pipe cleaner into a beak shape. Colour it in with black felt pen.

5

Use a sharp pencil to make three holes in the ball for the legs and neck. Push the legs and neck into the holes.

6

Cut out feather shapes from the pink paper. Glue them to the flamingo's body. Add the eye stickers.

Decorate the feathers with glitter for extra sparkle!

Keep out!

Make a sign to hang around the flamingo's neck

Also make... an ostrich
Follow the same steps, but use different-coloured materials.

cheetah

Give a friend a fright with this bright pop-out card!

 Some help needed

 30 minutes

  ★★

YOU WILL NEED

- 🐾 Card – thin green (A4), thin yellow, yellow strip (18 cm x 3 cm), scraps of assorted green
- 🐾 Coloured pencils
- 🐾 Eye stickers provided
- 🐾 Felt pen – black
- 🐾 Glue stick
- 🐾 Pencil
- 🐾 Ruler
- 🐾 Scissors

1 Fold the green card in half. Cut out leaf shapes from scraps of green card and glue them onto the front and inside.

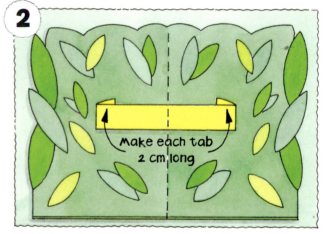

2 Make each tab 2 cm long

Fold the strip of yellow card in half, and fold tabs on each end. Stick the tabs inside the green card so the folds match up in the centre.

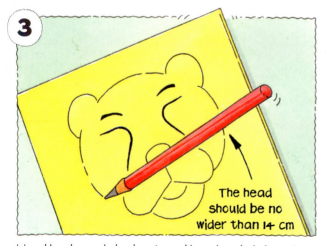

3 The head should be no wider than 14 cm

Use the template to draw the cheetah head and face outline on yellow card.

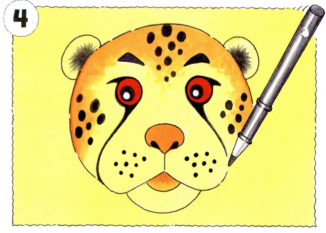

4 Draw the features with the black felt pen, then colour them in using coloured pencils. Add the eye stickers.

5

Run a ruler along the fold to make it extra firm

Cut out the face. Fold it in half, making a firm crease down the centre.

6

Glue the head to the card strip, matching up all three folds in the centre. Leave to dry.

Happy Birthday

write a special greeting on the front

SNARL!

Also make... a leopard
Follow the same steps, but give the big cat different features.

Monkey

See how many monkeys you can make for this crazy chain!

 Help not needed

 20 minutes

  ★

YOU WILL NEED

- Card – grey
- Coloured pencils – grey or silver, black
- Eye stickers provided
- Felt pen – black
- Pencil
- Scissors

1 Using the template, draw a monkey outline on the grey card.

Trace or copy the template

2 Cut out the shape.

3 Colour in the monkey's body on both sides using grey or silver pencils. Use different shades to add fur texture.

4 Colour in the face with dark grey or black.

5

Add the eye stickers. Draw the mouth, nostrils, fingers and toes with the black felt pen.

6

Repeat steps 1 to 5 to make lots of monkeys for your chain.

Hook the arms, legs and tails together

Also make...
lots of different coloured monkeys and hang them around your bedroom!

OOH-OOH-EEE-EEE!

Crocodile

Make a snappy hideaway for all of your secret things!

Some help needed

1.5 hours, plus drying time

★★★

YOU WILL NEED

- Acrylic paint – light green, dark green, pink
- Bubble wrap
- Card – thin white
- Card box (such as a toothpaste box)
- Felt pen – black
- Glue brush
- Paintbrush
- Pencil
- 2 polystyrene balls (2 cm)
- PVA glue
- Ruler
- Scissors
- Sticky tape

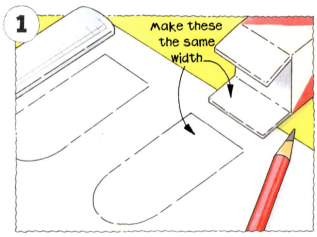

1 Make these the same width

Measure the width of the box flap. Draw two snout shapes on white card, the same width as the flap and 12 cm in length.

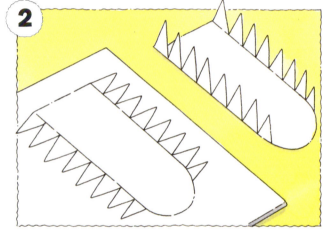

2 Along each snout length, draw zigzag teeth. Cut them out. Fold the teeth upwards.

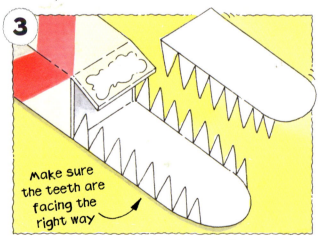

3 Make sure the teeth are facing the right way

Glue the snout shapes to the box flaps.

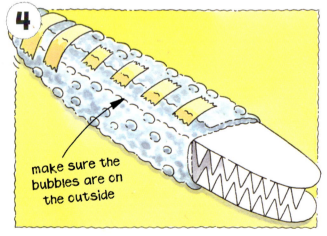

4 make sure the bubbles are on the outside

Tape bubble wrap tightly around the box, without covering the snout. Squeeze the far end into a tail shape.

5

Using the template, cut out two leg shapes. Glue them to the underside of the body.

6

Don't paint the teeth

Paint the body, snout and legs with dark-green paint. Add splodges of light-green paint. Paint the inside of the mouth pink. Leave to dry.

7

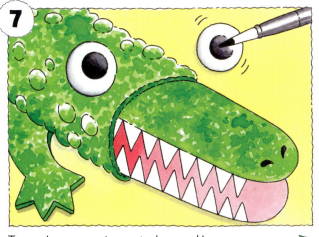

To make eyes, draw circles on the polystyrene balls with the black felt pen. Glue them to the body. Draw the nostrils.

Put your things inside the crocodile's body, through the mouth

SNAP! SNAP!

Hippopotamus

Keep your books in place with a heavy hippo bookend!

 Some help needed

 2 hours, plus drying time

YOU WILL NEED

- Acrylic paint – grey, pink, black
- Card – scraps of thick
- 4 card tubes (3 cm x 3 cm)
- Eye stickers provided
- Glue brush
- Masking tape
- Newspaper
- Paintbrush
- Paper towel
- Pebbles – 1 about 12 cm long, 1 about 8 cm long
- PVA glue
- Scissors

1 To make the body and head, cover the pebbles with layers of newspaper strips. Tape the paper tightly in place with masking tape.

2 Stuff the card tubes with newspaper, add glue to the ends and tape them to the body. Make sure the legs stand flat. Leave to dry.

The glue will make them stick better

3 Cut out two card ears and tape them to the head. Tape the head to the body.

4 Twist a piece of newspaper for the tail and glue it in place.

5 cover all of the joins

Glue small pieces of paper towel over the hippo's head, body and legs. Leave to dry.

6

Paint the hippo grey. Add pink paint to its face, legs and underside. Leave to dry. Paint the mouth and toes black and add the eye stickers.

Make two hippos to hold up each end of your row of books

Give your happy hippo a big grin

Also make... a rhino
Use the same steps, but add a twisted paper horn on its head, as well as a longer tail.

Python

Decorate your pens and pencils with slithering snakes!

 Help not needed

 20 minutes

  ★

YOU WILL NEED

- Bead (2 cm in diameter)
- Card – scraps of pink
- Eye stickers provided
- Glue brush
- Pencil
- Pipe cleaners – thick brown, thick cream
- PVA glue
- Scissors

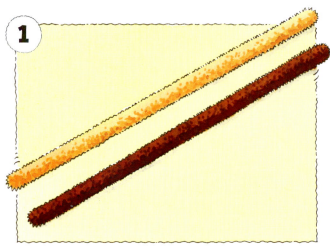

1 Line up the brown and cream pipe cleaners side by side.

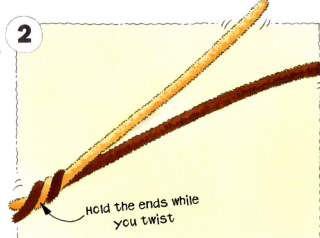

Hold the ends while you twist

2 Join the pipe cleaners at one end by twisting together tightly.

If the pipe cleaners are not tight enough, untwist and start again

3 Carefully twist them together along the whole length.

4 Add glue to one end of the twisted pipe cleaners and push the bead onto it. Leave to dry.

18

5

Add the eye stickers. Cut out a long forked tongue from the pink card. Add glue to the end and push it into the bead hole.

6

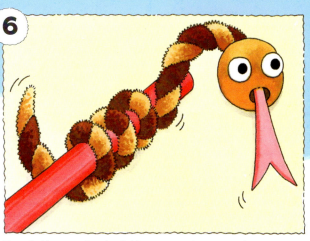

Twist the snake tightly around a pencil.

Also make... lots of snakes using different-coloured pipe cleaners.

Use bright-coloured pencils

HISS! HISS!

Parrot

Make a parrot mobile and watch its wings flap!

 Some help needed

 1 hour

  ★★

YOU WILL NEED

- Card – thin light grey (A4), thin grey, thin red
- Elastic – thin black
- Eye stickers provided
- Glue stick
- Pencil (sharp)
- Scissors

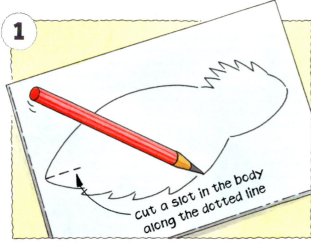

1

cut a slot in the body along the dotted line

Using the template, draw the parrot's body shape on light-grey card and cut it out.

2

Using the template, cut two beak shapes from the grey card and glue them to both sides of the face. Add the eye stickers.

3

cut a slot in the tail along the dotted line

Using the templates, draw two wings with tabs on the light-grey card. Draw a tail on the red card. Cut them out.

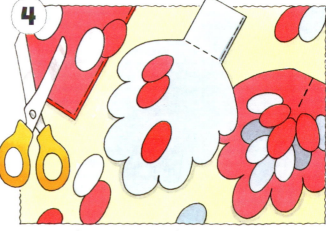

4

Cut out feather shapes from the spare red and grey card. Glue them onto the wings and tail.

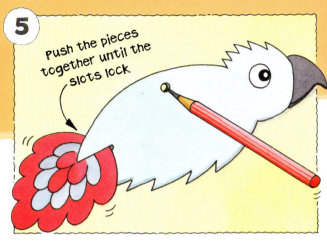

5 Push the pieces together until the slots lock

Slot the tail into the body. Using a sharp pencil, make a small hole in the top of the body. Thread the elastic through the hole.

6

Glue a wing to each side of the body using the tabs.

Hold the elastic and pull down on the parrot to see it flap its wings

SQUAWK!

Wild dog

Store your sweets inside this growling guard dog!

 Some help needed

 1.5 hours, plus drying time

  ★★★

YOU WILL NEED

- Acrylic paint – brown, yellow, black
- Card – light brown (A4)
- Card tube with lid (eg biscuit tube, 12 cm long)
- Eye stickers provided
- Felt pen – black
- Glue brush
- Paintbrush
- Pencil
- Pipe cleaner
- PVA glue
- Scissors

1 Using the templates, draw the body, neck, head, tail and base on brown card. Cut them out.

Use a pipe cleaner to hold the body in place while the glue dries

2 Fold the neck and legs along the dotted lines. Add glue to the body and wrap it around the tube. Glue the neck to the far end (not the lid).

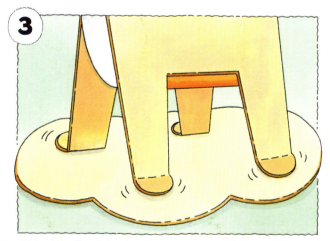

3 Glue the feet to the base and leave to dry.

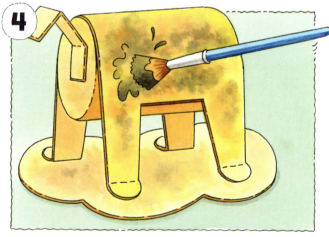

4 Paint the body with brown, yellow and black paint to give a mottled pattern. Paint the base and leave to dry.

5

Paint the face with black and yellow paint. Draw the nose and mouth with the black felt pen. Add the eye stickers.

6

Glue the head to the neck. Glue the tail to the lid.

Tap the head to see it nod up and down

Remove the lid to store your secret stash of sweets inside

GRRRR!

23

meerkat

Make a bookmark that pops up to say hello!

 Some help needed

 30 minutes

YOU WILL NEED

- Card – 2 strips of light brown (21 cm x 10 cm), 1 strip (10 cm x 4 cm)
- Coloured pencils
- Eye stickers provided
- Glue stick
- Pencil
- Ruler
- Scissors

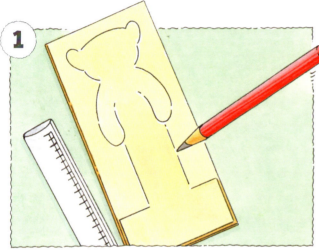

1 Using the template, draw the outline of a meerkat's head and bookmark shape on light-brown card.

cut along the arms but not across the body

2 Cut out the shape.

3 Using the template, draw and colour in the meerkat's face using coloured pencils. Add the eye stickers.

4 On the front of the other piece of card, draw a burrow and colour it in.

5

Add the glue in thin lines

Glue the edges of the small strip of card to the back of the burrow card. Leave to dry.

6

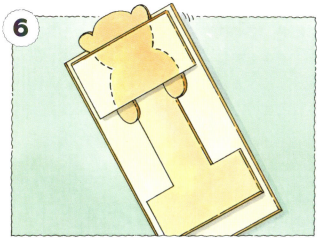

Tuck the meerkat underneath this strip. It should move up and down easily.

Hiding in its burrow

Push the meerkat right up and carefully pull it down, so the arms overlap the burrow

warthog

Keep your savings inside this special piggy bank!

YOU WILL NEED

 Help needed

 1 hour, plus drying time

  ★★★

- Acrylic paint – black, light grey, dark grey
- Card – thick white, scraps
- 4 card tubes (2.5 cm x 5 cm)
- Eye stickers provided
- Felt pen – black
- Glue brush
- Paintbrush
- Paper towel
- Pencil
- Plastic bottle (about 10 cm long)
- PVA glue
- Scissors
- Sticky tape

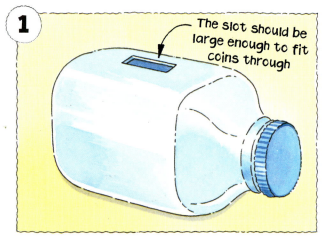

1

The slot should be large enough to fit coins through

Before you start, ask an adult to cut a slot in the side of the plastic bottle. This is the body.

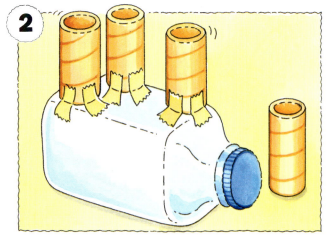

2

Tape the card tubes to the bottle on the opposite side to the slot. Make sure it stands up and doesn't wobble.

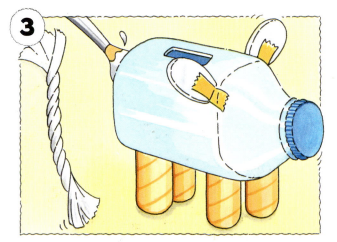

3

Cut out two card ears and tape them to the bottle. Make a tail from a twist of paper towel and glue it in place.

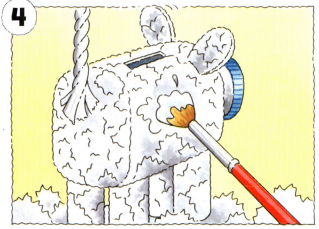

4

Glue small pieces of paper towel over the body and legs. Don't cover the slot or the bottle's lid (the nose). Leave to dry.

5

Mix black and white paint if you don't have grey

Paint the body light grey. Paint the ears, tail and nose dark grey. Paint the toes black. Leave to dry. Draw nostrils on the lid with black felt pen.

6

Using the template, draw four tusks on white card. Cut them out and glue to the head. Add the eye stickers.

Put coins in through the slot

Also make...
a farmyard pig by painting it pink instead of grey!

Get coins out by unscrewing the nose

OINK!

OINK!

Lion

Let the fearless lion protect your favourite photo!

 Help not needed

 1 hour, plus drying time

  ★★★

YOU WILL NEED

- Acrylic paint – light brown, dark brown
- Card – scraps of thick
- 4 card tubes (3 cm x 3 cm)
- Eye stickers provided
- Felt pen – black
- Glue brush
- Margarine tub with lid
- Masking tape
- Newspaper
- Paintbrush
- Pencil (sharp)
- Pipe cleaners – thick orange, thin orange, thin black
- PVA glue
- Scissors

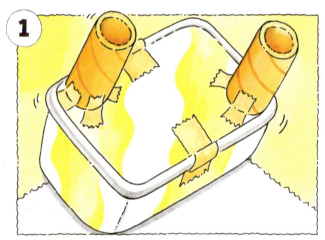

1

To make the body and legs, tape the lid to the tub. Then tape the card tubes to the lid.

2

Tightly scrunch a ball of newspaper and tape it to the body. Cut out two card ears and tape them to the head.

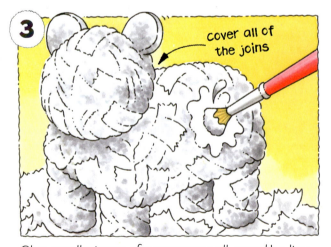

3

cover all of the joins

Glue small pieces of newspaper all over the lion. Leave to dry.

4

Paint the body and head light brown. Leave to dry. Paint the toes dark brown.

5

Add the eye and eyebrow stickers

Cut the black pipe cleaner into six pieces. Using a sharp pencil, make three holes in each side of the face. Push the pipe cleaners into the holes. Draw a mouth, nose and spots with the felt pen.

6

Bend the thick orange pipe cleaner around the lion's head. Twist the ends together and cut off any extra. Push the thin pipe cleaner into the end of the body for the tail.

stick your photo between the lion's ears and mane

ROOAAR!

Also make... a lioness
Follow the same steps, but use a smaller tub and don't add a mane.

Zebra

Give one of your friends a galloping greetings card!

 Some help needed

 30 minutes, plus drying time

  ★

YOU WILL NEED

- Acrylic paint – yellow
- Card – black, white
- Eye sticker provided
- Felt pen – black
- Glue stick
- Paintbrush
- Paper – green
- Paperclips
- Paper plate, or round piece of card
- Pencil
- Scissors

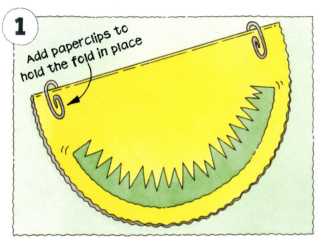

1 Add paperclips to hold the fold in place

Fold the paper plate in half. Paint it yellow and leave to dry. Cut out grass from the green paper and stick it to the plate.

2

Using the template, draw a galloping zebra on the white card and cut it out.

3

Colour in the stripes, hooves and nose with the black felt pen. Add an eye sticker.

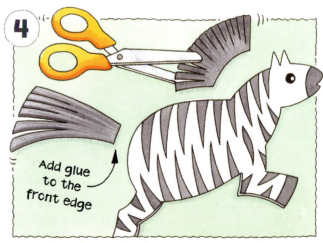

4 Add glue to the front edge

Using the template, draw a mane and tail on the black card. Cut out and snip along the dotted lines. Glue them in place.

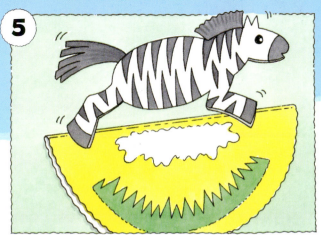

5

Glue the zebra to the plate, making sure that the legs don't sit too low. Open up the plate slightly to make it stand up.

Push down on the zebra's nose to make it gallop

write your message inside

CLIP! CLOP!

Also make...
a gazelle
You'll need light- and dark-brown card.

Lizard

Use this magnet to stick up your notes and photos!

 Help not needed

 40 minutes, plus drying time

  ★★

YOU WILL NEED

- Acrylic paint – orange, grey, white
- Card – white
- Eye stickers provided
- Felt pen – black
- Glue brush
- Kitchen foil (50 cm long)
- Magnet
- Paintbrush
- Paper towel
- Pencil
- PVA glue
- Scissors
- Stick (thin)

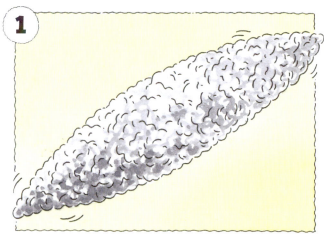

1

Scrunch the foil into a long oval shape to make the body. Pinch the ends into points.

2

Pinch the tail so it's thinner than the body

Shape the ends to make a head and tail. Gently press the stick across the tail to make grooves.

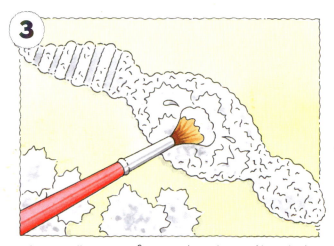

3

Glue small pieces of paper towel over the whole lizard. Leave to dry.

4

Using the template, draw the legs on white card. Glue them to the underside of the body.

5

Paint stripes of orange and grey along the body. Add a white stripe down the back. Leave to dry.

6

Draw nostrils with black felt pen and add the eye stickers. Glue the magnet to the tummy.

Stick the lizard to your fridge or radiator

Also make...
a group of lizards, using different-coloured paints, to scuttle around your house!

Giraffe

Make this box to store your trinkets and treasures!

 Some help needed

 2 hours, plus drying time

  ★★★

YOU WILL NEED

- Acrylic paint – yellow, brown
- Box (8 cm x 8 cm x 13 cm)
- Card (scraps)
- Card tube (15 cm x 3 cm)
- 4 card tubes (8 cm x 3 cm)
- Eye stickers provided
- Felt pen – black
- Glue brush
- Paintbrush
- Pencil
- Pipe cleaner – thin brown
- Polystyrene egg (8 cm)
- PVA glue
- Scissors
- Sticky tape
- 3 wooden beads (2 cm in diameter)

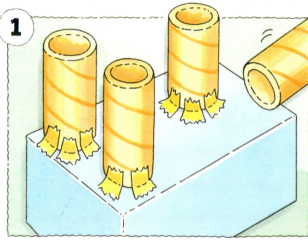

1 Tape the card tubes to the underside of the box. This is the body and legs. Turn over the box to make sure the legs are level.

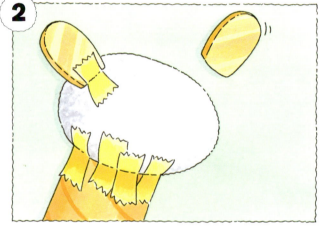

2 To make the head and neck, tape the polystyrene egg to the top of the long tube. Cut out two card ears and tape them to the head.

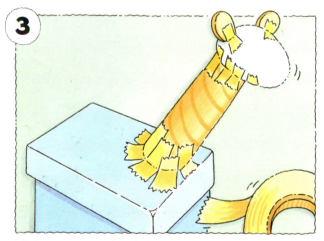

3 Make a diagonal cut through the other end of the long tube. Tape it to the lid of the box, so it sits at an angle.

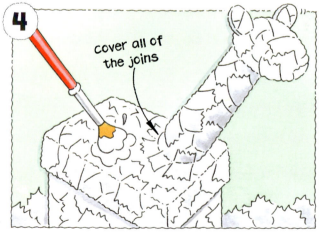

cover all of the joins

4 Glue pieces of newspaper on the whole model, but don't glue the lid to the box. Leave to dry.

5

Don't forget to paint inside the body

Paint the giraffe yellow. Use brown paint to add spots. Leave to dry.

6

Use the black felt pen to draw the nostrils and mouth. Add the eye stickers.

7

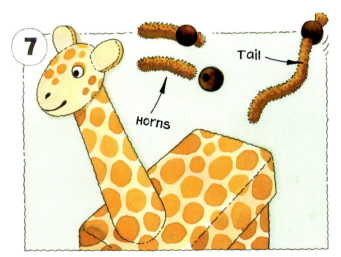

Tail

Horns

Cut the pipe cleaner into one long and two short pieces. Add a bead to each piece. Push the two short pieces into the head and the long piece into the end of the body.

Remove the lid to store your special things

Drawing templates

Use these templates to help you draw difficult shapes. You can either copy or trace them.

cheetah head

Monkey

warthog tusk

36

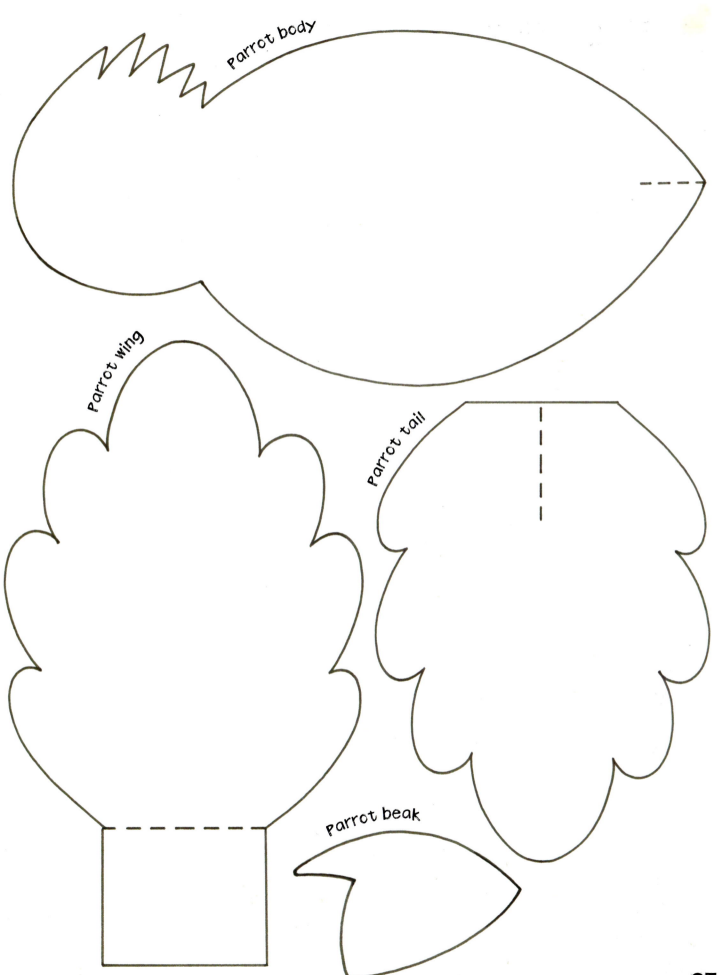

Parrot body

Parrot wing

Parrot tail

Parrot beak

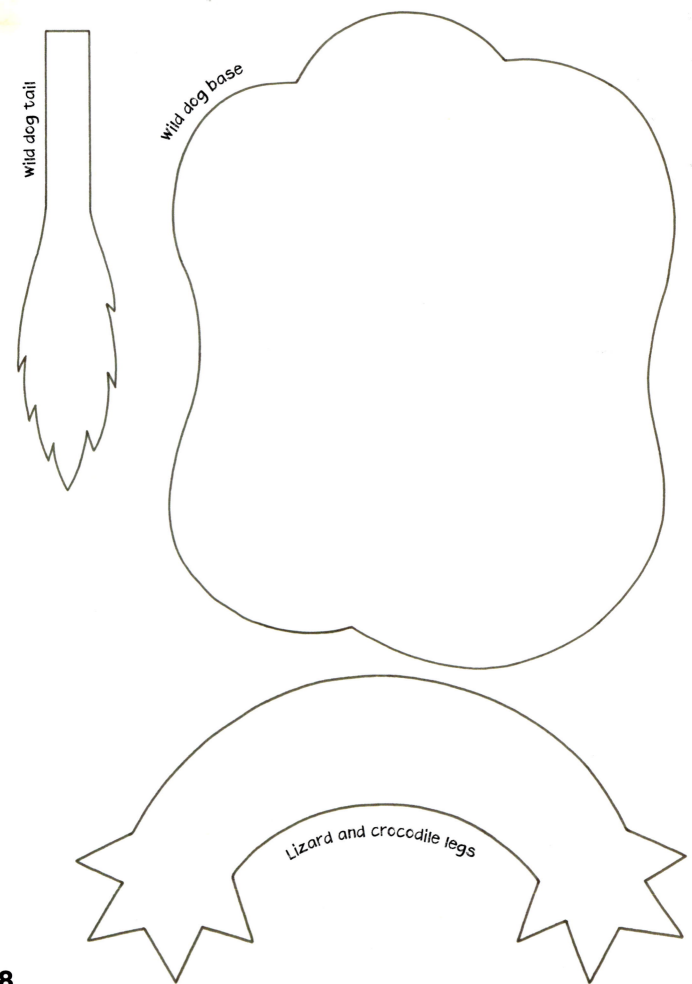

Wild dog tail

Wild dog base

Lizard and crocodile legs

38

wild dog body

wild dog head

Meerkat

wild dog neck

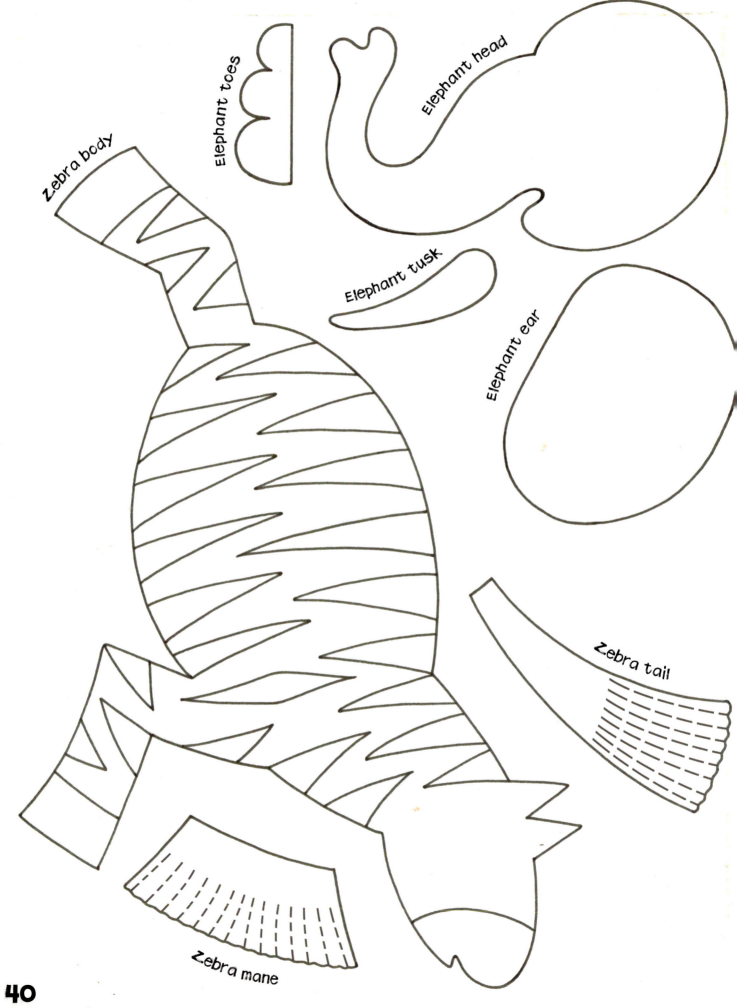

Elephant toes

Elephant head

Zebra body

Elephant tusk

Elephant ear

Zebra tail

Zebra mane

40

THE GREATCOAT

Helen Dunmore

In 1945, newlywed Isabel Carey arrives in a Yorkshire town with her husband Philip. One cold winter night, Isabel finds an old RAF greatcoat in the back of a cupboard. Once wrapped in the coat she is beset by dreams. And not long afterwards, while her husband is out, she is startled to hear a knock at her window, and to meet the intense gaze of a young Air Force pilot, staring in at her from outside. His name is Alec. As Isabel's initial alarm fades, they begin a delicious affair. But nothing could have prepared her for the truth about Alec's life . . .

THE BETRAYAL

Helen Dunmore

Leningrad in 1952: a city recovering from war, where Andrei, a young doctor and Anna, a school teacher, are forging a life together. Summers at the dacha, preparations for the hospital ball, work and the care of 16-year-old Kolya fill their minds. They try hard to avoid coming to the attention of the authorities, but even so their happiness is precarious. Stalin is still in power, and the Ministry for State Security has new targets in its sights. When Andrei has to treat the seriously ill child of a senior secret police officer he finds himself and his family caught in an impossible game — for in a land ruled by whispers and watchfulness, betrayal can come from those closest to you.